# Embracing Effulgence

GAIL Bhimsingh

BookLeaf Publishing

India | USA | UK

Presentation by *BookLeaf Publishing*

Web: www.bookleafpub.com

E-mail: info@bookleafpub.com

ISBN: 9789360948870

First edition 2024

*To Mia and Navya,*

*You are the heartbeats of my soul, the stars that guide me through the darkest nights, and the boundless source of love that fills my days with light. This book is dedicated to you, my beloved children, whose presence in my life ignites my spirit and fills my heart with endless joy. May its words serve as a reminder of the infinite depth of my love for you both, and may you always find solace, inspiration, and wonder within its pages.*

*With all my love,*

*Mummy*

# ACKNOWLEDGEMENT

With profound gratitude, I extend my heartfelt appreciation to my beloved children, Mia and Navya. Your unwavering love and encouragement are the driving forces behind my daily journey, inspiring me to embrace motherhood and humanity with boundless passion. You are my greatest blessing, and every moment spent with you is cherished beyond measure.

To my dear mother and sister, your quiet strength and unwavering support have fuelled my creative endeavours, allowing me to delve into the depths of my imagination with confidence and determination.

To my cherished friends, your constant support and enduring presence have been a source of immense joy and comfort throughout my journey. Your belief in me has been a guiding light, illuminating the path of my writing endeavours and enriching my life in countless ways.

And to Brent, my love, though you may not be physically present, your guidance and support have been a constant source of inspiration and strength. Your love continues to shape and uplift me, even in your absence.


With heartfelt appreciation and love,

Gail R. Bhimsingh

# PREFACE

In the quiet depths of our hearts lie stories of resilience, stories of enduring love, and stories of profound loss. This collection of poems is born from the intimate journey of a young mother thrust into the crucible of grief, her spirit tempered by the searing pain of loss and the relentless demands of single parenthood.

As the ink spills across these pages, it seeks to trace the contours of her grief-stricken path, a path shadowed by the untimely departure of her beloved husband to the merciless clutches of cancer. In the wake of this harrowing loss, she grapples with the weight of newfound responsibilities as a sole caregiver to her two precious daughters.

Yet amidst the darkness, there emerges a steadfast resolve – a resolve to honor her husband's memory not with tears of sorrow, but with the radiant light of joy that he brought into their lives. Through her unwavering determination, she endeavours to impart to her daughters the invaluable lesson that while grief may linger, it need not define their existence. Instead, they are urged to embrace life with a fervent tenacity, to seize each moment with unyielding courage, and to nurture their souls with the boundless beauty that surrounds them.

This anthology is more than a mere collection of verses; it is a testament to the indomitable human spirit, a beacon of hope for all who find themselves ensnared by the suffocating grip of trauma and grief. It is a reminder that within the shattered fragments of our souls, there resides a strength that is both enduring and resplendent – a strength that allows us to rise, phoenix-like, from the ashes of our despair and reclaim our rightful place in the tapestry of life.

May these poems serve as a guiding light through the darkest of nights, offering solace to those who mourn and inspiration to those who seek to forge a path toward healing and redemption.

With love, light, and compassion

Gail R. Bhimsingh

# Twilight descends

I watched you intently,
As you walked around…
Your footsteps were slower today,
You said little; no sound

Your energy was low,
And you were so weak…
Yet you never complained,
About the pain; so deep

I watched you intently,
And I tried to help…
To help make you comfortable,
To ease some of the pain you felt

I watched as you winced,
When the pain became so sharp…
You twisted and you turned,
Watching you in distress became hard

I tried to help you,
Following all the instructions…
All that was prescribed for you,
Was supposed to ease your condition

As you tried to get some sleep,
I watched you get a little relief…
From all the discomfort,
And from the intense pain beneath

In one single minute
When I looked out…
I saw the unimaginable,
I saw the lights off!

You left without warning,
You seemed to have had enough…
I stared in complete disbelief,
Twilight descended as your light went off.

# Shattered

My gaze was fixed
I could not move
I watched your face
Not knowing what to do

A million prayers
Played in my mind
Yet not one sound
Could I define

My world was shattered
This feeling surreal
I felt so numb
My heart appealed

I tried to wake you
Talk and pray
But I got no response
You didn't even sway

A searing deep pain
Shot through my soul
I was completely broken
An abyss became my world!

# Perpetual Sadness

In this darkness of despair
My heart is full of sorrow
I'm overwhelmingly broken
How do I face tomorrow?

A tomorrow not seeing you smile
A tomorrow not hearing you speak
Not seeing the light in your eyes
Or even kissing your cheek

My thoughts cannot stop replaying
Those last and most crushing moments
When you stood around us
Exuding your light and presence

How do I console myself?
How suddenly it all happened
In one moment you were here
And Now; I'm sobbing; so overwhelmed

Sadness now fills my vision
Sadness has become my darkness
Sadness has engulfed my heart
Profound sadness has become my prison!

# In the Wake of Tears

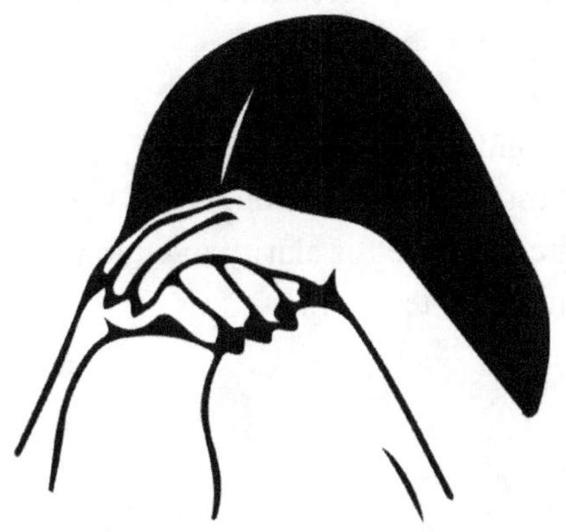

Crushing moments, devastated heart
Knocking the wind out of my chest
Disbelief; numbness
I, dry my own tears…..

In the stillness, in my space
In the darkness, an isolated place
I sob and crunch down, yet
I, dry my own tears……

No real support, no true friends
Does loyalty exist; does the pain ever end?
I look up to the vast sky and still
I, dry my own tears…..

I wait, I pray, I wait, I meditate
I feel this piercing pain of grief
Feeling every cell screaming each second
I, dry my own tears……

I stare blankly into the horizon
Uncertain about inner strength
I ask the universe for clarity over confusion as
I, dry my own tears…..

# The Quiet Void

I see only the present
This moment and Today
My mind focuses on the now
What lies immediately in my way…..

I feel safe in isolation
Not wanting anyone around
So I can sink into despair
Into blinding darkness; no sound…..

I don't want to pretend anymore
To make them feel better
I want to cry and sob
Now nothing else matters…..

Let me stay in my silence
Let me withdraw within
Let me meet my pain completely
Surrender to it; therein…..

# Grief Unbound

Into the stillness of the night
My thoughts are racing
Scenarios playing…
Of you, alive well and smiling

I get up suddenly
Having difficulty to breathe,
As my mind fails to comprehend
Your absence from me...

This truth is difficult
My heart fights to accept
That you are really gone
Taken away; death…

How does anyone…
Come to accept reality?
My days go by like fleeting dreams
Your absence; a harsh finality!

# Lost

These days pass slowly
The months have rolled by,
Watching life flicker in slow motion
Feeling lost; lost inside…

Going through the motions
Putting up a play,
So that the people around me
Would feel better each day…

My mind feels numb
To the many daily distractions,
I feel lost inside
And I have no reaction…

I am unsure about forever
I question this life,
I question the promises
That has made me paralyzed…

This grief overwhelms
My heart and my soul,
I am barely surviving
After death rocked my world…


There is no present direction
No goal, no aim,
Just moving one step at a time
And staying lost in my lane…

# Numbed Reverie

Listening to the sounds of insects
As they make midnight music,
Their routine is certain
Their presence; cryptic…

As dawn approaches again
Welcoming another day,
I reflect on myself
And this numbness that stays…

Hoping that the passage of time
Diminishes this stagnancy,
Of numbness, indifference
Death ; agony…

I set this intention
To accept that it happened,
To practice forgiveness
And let my inner self strengthen…

# Introspection

I go within…
Within my soul
To observe, to search
To accept me; whole…

I explore, I find
Great sadness, great pain
Sitting there grounded
Unattended, unstained…

I explore, I find
Guilt and fear
Settled so deeply
Hidden but there…

I explore, I find
Impatience and anger
Unleashed, unsettling
Signals of danger

I become, I sit
Aware of it all
Acknowledging, Accepting
Feeling; No wall!

To heal my soul
I sit with these feelings,
Spend time, release
A catharsis to my well-being…

# Gone...Ever Present

Your face, Your eyes
In the raindrops, In my reflection
Through the lens of the sky
Gone…Ever present…

Your smile, Your laughter
I hear with clarity
Your touch, softer
Gone…Ever present…

Your hugs so safe
Your presence missed
Your voice, your sense of humor
Gone…Ever present…

I search tirelessly
To connect, to feel
The essence of you
Gone…Ever present…

My heart, My soul
Breaks; Cries
Your love for life
Gone…Ever Present…


You are greatly missed
Your heart, Your peace
Your shining bright light
Gone…Ever present…

# Crossroads Cadence

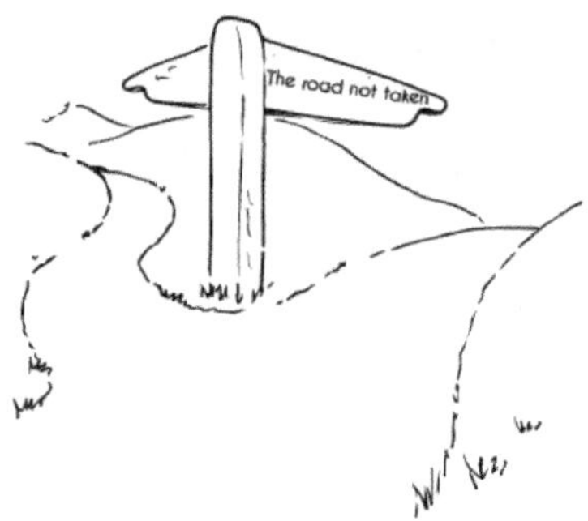


As the seasons changed
From dry and brown
To Shades of green
Saplings growing from the ground…

I have witnessed each moment
Every hour, every day…
Observing minute changes
Of my life in every way…

Living in this moment
Has become my accepted truth
I live in the now
Where I decide to consciously choose...

Do I choose to remain
Fixated on my past?
Or do I craft a future?
Bringing clarity to my abstract...

There is an unsettling fear
Arising out of my ordeal
What are my options really
Grim despair or Heal!

# The Inner Voice

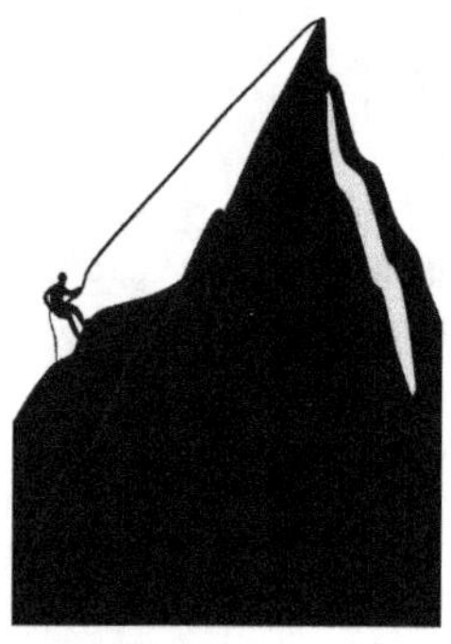

Have faith ….
That amidst the turmoil and trials
Of the past and the now
The light of the creator
Shines within thou…

The chaos will confuse you
And your focus may waiver
But shift…shift…
Be intentional, be calmer…

Have faith …..
No matter how difficult it may seem
You will come through this
Let it go, let the divine take the lead…

Have faith….
Remember that the universe supports you
You are blanketed with love
Through family friends and angels too!

# Sacred Stillness

In the depth of the stillness
So many questions arise
About life, about living
Our experiences,  Why?

In the depth of the stillness
Are intuitive whispers
Answers from our souls
Am I a Listener?

In the depth of the stillness
With each breath, I feel
The cells of my body
In tandem with my energy

In the depth of the stillness
I am guided to understand
Being part of the Divine
I Will, I Can, I Am

# Fragmented Realities

In exploring this confusion
I had to engage the pause
To become aware and mindful
To examine the present cause…

My sorrow and my anger
My laughter, cheerfulness, and hope
My irritation and impatience
Facing the confusion to cope…

I believed healing to be linear
It certainly is not to be…
My everyday encounter with mixed intense
emotions
Leaves me treading through carefully!

# "No" to Heal

In this journey back to peace
In this path to light…
Facing the discomfort
Was essentially a fight…

The unease of abuse
By multiple narcissists…
Has strengthened my inner warrior
My inner artist, my inner phoenix…

One word has held great power
To keep the negativity at bay…
'No' is one sentence
It is enough without debate…

'No' is a decision
'No' is complete…
A complete and whole answer
That does not require repeat…

"No" requires zero justification
Explanation or reasoning…
But letting go of all guilt
Insecurity and old conditioning!

# Acceptance

Acceptance means…
To acknowledge it is ok
Ok to the deep-seated grief
That resurfaces on an odd day

Acceptance means…
To feel joy fully...
Letting go of the guilt
And embrace smiles purely

Acceptance means…
That fear will threaten
Will overwhelm and cripple
Make you feel broken

Acceptance means…
That despite the fear
I will forge ahead
I am switching gears!

# Reassurance from Within

When the clouds get dark
And despair looms
Remember that one blessing...
Know that you are supported

When you fall flat
And weep all day
Remember you can breathe...
Know that you are supported

When all doors close
And you feel lost
Take those tiny steps forward...
Know that you are supported

When your world seems to be crashing
All is not lost
The presence of just one life...
Know that you are supported

The Divine supports you
Presently, Constantly
In your peak times and when you're low...
Do you see it? Can you feel it?

For know that there always is
And always will be
A purpose, A solution
To the problems, the disruptions

Know that you are supported
Through sunlight, through water
That nourishes you and the earth
Not discriminating; Prosper!

# Beginnings

As the sun peeps out
Of the clouds at dawn
A realization emerges
About life; moving on…

It is ok.…
Ok to feel
Feeling grief today
So deep, unconcealed…

It is ok…
Today to smile
Or even laugh heartily
Amidst all life's trials…

Even with tears glistening
In these soulful eyes
I remind myself
It is ok to smile…

It is ok…
Is the message that prevails
To the survivor; the warrior
In the rear-view mirror; setting sail…

# Ruminations of the Mind

As this chapter ends
Leaving behind a trail of emotions
Losing Loved ones , pain and heartbreak
Moving on to a new horizon

In stillness I focus
On feeling, on healing
I am aware of my pain
Transforming then releasing

I remember those kind souls
Who listened without judgement
Willing to help and empathetic
Thank you for your encouragement

I am grateful for strength
Strength of mind and, of soul
Strength to fall apart
To re-group.........and be whole

I thank the cells
Of my body, entirely
Despite many trying days,
They supported me, unconditionally

As this new chapter awaits
I consciously choose to...
Take responsibility for myself
My vision to pursue...

I thank this present moment
And those who are with me
For your continuous love and support
Being part of my reality!

# Whispers of Comfort

A time will come
For all to know
Of your presence, your energy
Your healing touch, your glow

The impact of your words
You are sometimes unaware
Is that one saving line
Bringing a healing touch to those in despair

Checking in , Listening
Are two priceless gifts
That cannot be bought
Your healing touch , It is

Those who received your smile
And perhaps didn't tell you
It has brought comfort and consolation
Your healing touch ; faith renewed

You seem not to know
That your kindness is treasured
Your presence , a blessing
Your healing touch , unmeasured

You have restored hope and healing
To so many different lives,
This message is to let You know my friend
Your healing touch is from the Divine!

# Unapologetic Authenticity

This is Me...
Healthy, Motivated, Striving
I choose to live
Despite falling, despite breaking

This is Me...
My words are raw, unfiltered
Open and Direct
Speaking my truth; not bothered

This is Me...
Stepping up and stepping out
From all the nonsensical drama
I'm blazing forward, without a doubt

This is Me...
Healing my chain of repeated patterns
For women of past generations
Breaking the cycle of suppression

This is Me...
Showing up, not shutting up
My words, my feelings matter!
No reservation, no discomfort

This is Me...
I embrace my wholeness
Accepting my moments present
I forge forward to live my future life…
UNAPOLOGETIC!!!

www.ingramcontent.com/pod-product-compliance
Lightning Source LLC
Chambersburg PA
CBHW061726130726
47996CB00006B/2526